Landmark Cases of Indian Judiciary

TO THE PEOPLE,

THOSE WHO INSPIRED ME.

ACKNOWLEDGEMENT

Writing a book is harder than I thought and more rewardable than I expect the reward. None of this became possible without our friends and family they stood us during at every struggle done by us. I am eternally grateful to my college friends, who took in an extra mouth to feed when he didn't have to. They taught me discipline, tough love, manners, respect, and so much more that has helped me succeed in life. I truly have no idea where I had been they hadn't given us a roof over our head or became the father figure whom I desperately needed at that age.

Writing a book about **Landmark Cases Of Indian Judiciary** is like to do social service which is like a surreal process. I found no words to express our sense of gratitude towards our parents for providing the necessary guidance and constant encouragement at every step of their endeavour. I am extremely grateful to my respected teachers of the School of Law-Manipal University, Jaipur for their co-operation and guidance and their valuable time. I am highly indebted to the office and library staff of the college for the support in cooperation extended by them from time to time.

Having an idea and turning it into a book is as hard as it sounds. The experience is both internally challenging and rewarding. I especially want to thank the individuals that helped make this happen.

<u>**I want to thank my :**</u>

- Parents
- Teachers
- Grandma.
- All my brothers and sisters.
- My best friends
- Department of the court system for giving the judgement to us.
- I want to thank EVERYONE who ever said anything positive to me or taught me something. I heard it all, and it meant something.
- I want to thank God most of all because without God I wouldn't be able to do any of this.

<u>Preface</u>

I Being a Law student makes me responsible for contributing towards this cause and enlightening people about, The most prominent cases of the Indian Judiciary.

The work contains a detailed analysis form the head to tail in a sequential way as the events unfolded and would help you get a broad overview of the subject matter.

I have not been Judge mental while expressing my views it's a decision which I have left for the reader to decide based on their prudence.

As stated by Jeremy Bentham **'greatest good for the greatest number'** I Hope the reader would keep the following in the mind before conclu**ding.**

Regards,

Siddhartha Kundoo

(Author)

 Ph. No. +91 7424913711

siddharthakundoo5@gmail.com

https://m.facebook.com/MAVESID?ref=bookmarks

Contents

Introduction

The Constitution of India became effective on the 26th Of January, 1950, and is the spring of law and the incomparable law of India. The court framework where debates are settled, choices are made by a seat of judges or officers, and the law is implemented is known as the Judiciary System. The Judges and the justices structure the centre of the Judiciary.

The Judiciary of India is stratified into numerous levels and takes after a pyramid with the Supreme Court at its peak.

•It is a coordinated framework and the choices made by the higher courts are authoritative on the lower courts.

•It is likewise a redrafting framework. Each resident of India has the option to interest a higher court if discontent with the judgment of the lower court.

Here is a fast look at the Judiciary of India in the plummeting request:

Supreme Court

The Supreme Court was built upon the 28th of January, 1950. Situated in the capital of India, New Delhi, this court is the most noteworthy legal assemblage of India, and according to the Constitution, it is the most elevated court of a claim. The Supreme Court situates the Chief Justice of India alongside 30 different judges for warning purview. Every one of the judges of the Supreme Court is chosen by the President of India. Incomparable Court manages uncertain cases and cases in a debate. The request for the Supreme Court is the last word and it is official on the courts of the considerable number of States and Union domains.

High Courts

The High Court comes next in the line of a chain of importance. According to the Constitution of India, each State ought to have a High Court. The High Court manages common just like criminal cases. The Judges of the High Court are selected by the President of India in discussion with the Chief Justice of India and the legislative head of the State concerned. The Calcutta High Court, built up in the year 1862, is the most established in India and has the ward over the province of Its Bengal and Union Territory of Andaman and Nicobar Islands.

District Courts

Legal issues at the locale level of a State are managed by the District Courts. They are the subordinate courts to the High Court according to the Constitution of India and in this manner are authoritatively and judicially constrained by the High Court. The District Courts have a few optional courts under them as per the populace appropriation of the State. It is going by a judge.

Lok Adalat

The Judiciary System of India additionally incorporates the Lok Adalat. Given the elective debate goals, this court effectively resolves issues between two gatherings genially by method for a trade-off. The Lok Adalat is sorted out by any of the accompanying three:

•High Court Legal Services Committee

•District Legal Services Authority

•Taluk Legal Services Committee

The Judiciary System of India assumes a significant job as the caretaker of the Constitution of India by protecting the principal privileges of the resident of India.

Judiciary in India: 11 Salient Features of Indian Judiciary

The Constitution of India accommodates a solitary coordinated legal framework with the Supreme Court at the summit, High Courts at the centre (state) level and District Courts at the nearby level. It additionally accommodates a free and ground-breaking legal framework. Legal executive in India goes about as the watchman defender of the Constitution and the major privileges of the individuals.

Striking Features of Indian Judiciary:

1. Single and Integrated Judicial System:

The Constitution sets up a solitary coordinated legal framework for the entire of India. The Supreme Court of India is the most elevated court of the nation and underneath it is the High Courts at the state level. Different courts (Subordinate Courts) work under the High Courts. The Supreme Court controls and runs the legal organization of India. All courts in India structure connections of a solitary legal framework.

2. The autonomy of Judiciary:

The Constitution of India makes legal executive genuinely autonomous. It accommodates:

(I) Appointment of judges by the President,

(ii) High capabilities for arrangement as judges,

(iii) Removal of judges by a troublesome technique for reprimand,

(iv) High pay rates, annuity and other administration benefits for judges,

(v) Independent foundation for the Judiciary, and

(vi) Adequate forces and useful self-governance for the Judiciary.

Every one of these highlights together makes the Indian Judiciary an autonomous legal executive.

3. Legal executive as the Interpreter of the Constitution:

The Constitution of India is composed and authorized. The privilege to decipher and explain the Constitution has been given to the Supreme Court. It is the last mediator of the arrangements of the Constitution of India.

4. Legal Review:

The Constitution of India is the preeminent tradition that must be adhered to. The Supreme Court goes about as the mediator and defender of the Constitution. It is the watchman of the principal rights and opportunities of the individuals. For playing out this job, it practices the intensity of legal audit. The Supreme Court can decide the sacred legitimacy all things considered. It can dismiss any such law which is held to be unlawful.

5. High Court for every state also a Provision for Joint High Courts:

The Constitution sets out that there is to be a High Court for each state. Be that as it may, at least two states can, by common assent, have a Joint High Court.

6. Preeminent Court as the Arbiter of lawful questions between the Union and States:

The Constitution provides for the Supreme Court the ward in all instances of questions:

(I) Between the Government of India and at least one states,

(ii) Between the Government of India and any state or states on one side and at least one states on the other, and

(iii) Between at least two states.

7. The watchman of Fundamental Rights:

Indian legal executive goes about as the watchman of key rights and opportunities of the individuals. The individuals reserve the Privilege to Constitutional Remedies under which they can look for the insurance of the courts for averting an infringement or for gathering any danger to their privileges. The Supreme Court and the High Courts can issue writs for this reason.

8. Partition of Judiciary from the Executive:

The Constitution of India accommodates a partition between the legal executive and the other two organs of the legislature. The legal executive is neither a part of the official nor in any capacity subordinate to it. The legal organization in India is organised and kept running as per the principles and requests of the Supreme Court.

9. Open Trial:

The courts in India are free. These direct open preliminaries. The blamed is constantly given a full chance to shield himself. The state gives a free legitimate guide to poor people and penniless.

10. Legal Activism:

Indian Judicial System has been winding up increasingly dynamic. The Supreme Court has been turning out with legal choices and orders for dynamic security of open intrigue and human rights. The legal executive has been offering orders to open authorities for guaranteeing superior security for the privileges of general society. The Public Interest Litigation framework has been grabbing. The arrangement of Lok Adalats has likewise taken an appropriate shape and Ill being.

11. Open Interest Litigation System:

Under this framework, the official courtrooms in India can start and uphold activity for verifying any huge open or general intrigue which is as a rule antagonistically influenced or is probably going to be so by the activity of any office, open or private. Under it, any resident or a gathering or a deliberate association, or even a court herself, can bring to see any case requesting activity for ensuring and fulfilling an open intrigue.

It accommodates a simple, basic, speedier and more affordable arrangement of giving legal alleviation to the distressed open. With every one of these highlights, the Indian Judicial System is an autonomous, fair, free, ground-breaking and proficient legal framework

K. M. Nanavati v. State of Maharashtra was a 1959 Indian court situation where Kawas Manekshaw Nanavati, a Naval Commander, was gone after for the homicide of Prem Ahuja, his better half's darling. The occurrence got remarkable media inclusion and propelled a few books and motion pictures. Nanavati was at first announced not blameworthy by a jury, however, the decision was expelled by the Bombay High Court and the case was retried as a seat preliminary. The case was the last to be heard as a jury preliminary in India, as the legislature annulled jury preliminaries because of the case.

Proclamation of Problem

For this situation when the blame had applied before the senator for acquitting of his discipline and simultaneously he has applied for the intrigue in the Supreme Court against the choice of the High Court. To this SC rejected the appeal on the ground that both (governors poor and SC request) can't go on together.

Objective

The goal of this undertaking is: By contemplating this case I need to know the constraint/extent of Art. 161 and 142.

Speculation

Both the strategy can cooperate as both are of various fields.

The extent of The Study

The exploration is doctrinal research. The specialist here might want to find out about the punitive angle in this unique circumstance. The scientist has attempted to examination the theme by considering different writers, specialists, instances of The Indian Apex Court and High courts, articles, and so on. The analyst has carefully pursued the limit and has examined distinctly regarding Indian creators, specialists, cases, and so on.

Philosophy

The present research study is, for the most part, a doctrinal and logical. Keeping this in view, the analyst has experienced various books, diaries, Ib references, E-diary, reports and so on.

The applicable material is gathered from the optional sources. Materials and data are gathered both lawful sources like books.

Brief Facts of the case

The charged, Nanavati, at the hour of the supposed homicide, was second in order of the Indian Naval Ship "Mysore". He Added Sylvia in 1949 and had three kids. Since the hour of marriage, the couple Ire inhabiting better places having respect to the exigencies of administration of Nanavati. At long last, they moved to Bombay.

In a similar city, the expired Ahuja was working together in autos and the year 1956, Agniks, who Ire regular companions of Nanavati's and Ahujas, acquainted Ahuja and his sister with Nanavati's. Ahuja was unmarried and was around 34 years old at the hour of his demise.

Nanavati, as a Naval Officer, was oftentimes leaving from Bombay in his ship, leaving his better half and kids in Bombay. Progressively, a fellowship created among Ahuja and Sylvia, which finished in unlawful closeness between them.

On April 27, 1959, Sylvia admitted to Nanavati of her illegal closeness with Ahuja. Chafed at the lead of Ahuja, Nanavati Int to his ship, took from the stores of the ship a self-loader gun and six cartridges on a bogus guise, stacked the equivalent, Int to the level of Ahuja Int into his bedroom and shot him dead.

From that point, the denounced gave up himself to the police. He was put collared and at the appointed time he was focused on the Sessions for confronting a charge under s. 302 of the Indian Penal code.

Be that as it may, the resistance form was that the charged was away with his ship from April 6, 1959, to April 18, 1959. Following coming back to Bombay, he and his better half to Ahmednagar for around three days. From there on, they came back to Bombay and the denounced saw that his significant other was carrying on peculiarly and was not responsive or warm to him. Whenever addressed, she used to sidestep the issue.

Around early afternoon on April 27, 1959, when they Ire sitting in the living room for the lunch to be served, the denounced put his arm around his significant other warmly, when she appeared to go tense and lethargic.

After lunch, when he examined her concerning her constancy, she shook her head to demonstrate that she was unfaithful to him. He speculated that her lover was Ahuja. As she didn't show obviously whether Ahuja would Id her and take care of the kids, he chose to settle the issue with him. Sylvia begged him not go to Ahuja's home, as he may shoot him.

From that point, he drove his significant other, two of his kids and a neighbour's kid in his vehicle to a film, dropped them there and told to come and get them at 6 P.M. at the point when the show finished. He at that point drove his vehicle to his ship, as he needed to get medication for his wiped out pooch, he spoke to the experts in the ship, that he needed to draw a pistol and six rounds from the stores of the ship as he was going to drive alone to Ahmednagar by night, however, the genuine reason for existing was to shoot himself.

On getting the gun and six cartridges, and put it inside a darker envelope. At that point he drove his vehicle to Ahuja's office, and not discovering him there, he headed to Ahuja's level, extend the entryway chime, and, when it was opened by a hireling, strolled to Ahuja's bed-room, Int into the bed-room and shut the entryway behind him.

He likewise conveyed with him the envelope containing the pistol. The charged saw the perished inside the bed-room, considered him a squalid swine and asked him whether he would Id Sylvia and take care of the kids. The perished countered, "Am I to Id each lady I lay down with?" The blamed ended up chafed, put the envelope containing the pistol on a cupboard close by, and took steps to whip the expired.

The perished made an abrupt move to get a handle on at the envelope when the charged whipped out his pistol and instructed him to get back. A battle followed between two and during that battle two shots Int off coincidentally and hit Ahuja bringing about his passing. After the shooting, the denounced returned to his vehicle and drove it to the police headquarters where he gave up himself.

The trial court indicted under S.304 An of IPC and in a request, the high court convert it into S.302 of IPC.

So the denounce made an intrigue before the SC and simultaneously he made an application to senator under Art.161.

Issues in setting with an understanding of resolution

1. Whether SLP can be engaged without satisfying the request under Art. 142?

2. Whether the acquitting intensity of representative and SLP can be moved together?

Ans to issue 1

The SLP was expelled by the incomparable court, by larger part, holding that the appealing party's SLP couldn't be listed for hearing except if he gives up under Art. 142 (according to the judgment of HC).

Ans to issue 2

The litigant has made SLP and use of absolving capacity to the representative. The representative diminished his sentence. The SC held that SLP and exonerating force can't work together both are unique. If SLP is recorded, at that point, the intensity of senator in such condition will be stopped.

 Further court held that the Art.142 and 161 are distinctive. The two Articles are reconcilable and ought to be accommodated. The standard of statutory conjunction expressed that it is once in a while discovered that the 2 resolution struggle, as their goal is extraordinary and language of each is limited to its item or subject, so they run parallel and never meet.

No standard of development can necessitate that when the expressions of a rule pass on the unmistakable importance, it will be important to present another piece of the resolution which talk with less perspicuity and of which the word might be prepared to do such development as by probability to decrease the adequacy of the other arrangement of the Act.

Under Art. 142 except if the request for lower-court doesn't pursue SC may not engage the SLP and in Art. 145 courts have all the capacity to make the Law to give equity.

Judgment

The perished allured the spouse of the charged. She had admitted to him of her illegal closeness with the expired. It was characteristic that the blamed was irritated at the directions for the perished and had, in this way, adequate rationale to get rid of the expired. He intentionally verified the gun on a bogus guise from the ship, headed to the level of Ahuja, Int into his bed-room unceremoniously with a stacked gun close by and in around a couple of moments from there on turned out with the gun in his hand. The perished was discovered dead in his restroom with projectile wounds on his body. It isn't questioned that the shots that made wounds Ahuja exuded from the pistol that was in the hand of the denounced. After the shooting, until his preliminary in the Sessions Court, he didn't tell anyone that he shot the perished coincidentally. Without a doubt, he admitted his blame to the chowkidar Puransingh and conceded the equivalent to his associate Samuel. His depiction of the battle in the restroom is exceptionally fake and is without every single fundamental specific. The wounds found on the body of the perished are reliable with the deliberate shooting and the fundamental wounds are completely conflicting with unintentional shooting when the person in question and the attacker Ire in close grasps. Different conditions brought out in the proof additionally set up that there couldn't have been any battle or battle between the blamed and the perished.

The court held that the lead of the charged demonstrates that the homicide was a conscious and determined one and the realities of the case don't pull in the arrangements of Exceptions 1 of Sec 300 of IPC as the denounced likewise neglected to bring the case under General Exception of IPC by citing proof. In the outcome, the conviction of the blamed under area 302 for IPC and condemned him of detainment forever.

Conclusion

From this, I can say the exacting guideline has been applied to the court and simply read the plain content of the constitution which utilized by the SC for this situation. Just on the disappointment of strict principle different standards of translation can be utilized. Be that as it may, the law is clear thus there is no point of applying some other principle. The choice of the Supreme Court is impeccable as indicated by me in this case. There is no issue that 2 cure can't be allowed for one reason and the same thing is laid down here.

What is the long-standing Ayodhya/Ram Mandir contest about?

It comes down to a plot of land in the city of Ayodhya in Uttar Pradesh. The site that is viewed among Hindus as the origination of Lord Rama additionally verifiably finds Babri Mosque. Presently whether a past Hindu sanctuary was crushed or changed to make the mosque is an inquiry.

The contention of history

As indicated by the Hindus, the arrive on which the Babri mosque was worked in 1528 is the 'Smash Janmabhoomi' (origin of the god-ruler Rama). Be that as it may, Mir Baqi, one of Mughal ruler Babur's commanders, is said to have crushed a prior sanctuary of Rama and constructed a mosque called Babri Masjid (Babur's mosque) at the site.

Both the networks have loved at the "mosque-sanctuary", Muslims inside the mosque and Hindus outside it. Be that as it may, in 1885 an appeal was documented by the leader of the

Nirmohi Akhara requesting authorization to offer petitions to Ram Lalla inside what was known as the Babri Masjid.

The consent was not given yet in 1886, area Judge of Faizabad court FEA Chamier gave his decision and stated, "It is most heartbreaking that a masjid ought to have been based ashore uniquely held hallowed by the Hindus, however as that occasion happened 356 years prior, it is past the point of no return currently to cure the complaint."

It was in 1950 that a nearby occupant Gopal Singh Visharad documented a grumbling in the common courts mentioning authorization to offer supplications in the mosque where the symbols Ire introduced.

Court's decision

The Allahabad High Court managed the contested land in Ayodhya will be isolated into three sections. The 2.77 sections of land will be separated between Hindus, Muslims and the Nirmohi Akhara. A seat of Justices Aftab Alam and R.M. Lodha remained the September 30, 2010 judgment of the Lucknow Bench of the High Court in the wake of conceding a bunch of bids from both Hindu and Muslim associations. The seat considered the decision by the Allahabad High Court as 'odd' as no gathering appealed to God for it.

The Bench said existing conditions at the contested site would stay as coordinated by the 1994 Constitution Bench and the request passed on March 13-14, 2002.

Ongoing improvements

Prior this year Vishwa Hindu Parishad (VHP) reported an across the country drive to gather stones for the development of the Ram sanctuary in Ayodhya. As of late, two trucks of stones landed in the city and the leader of Ram Janam Bhumi Nyas, Mahant Nritya Gopal Das told PTI there was a "signal" from the Modi government to construct the sanctuary "now".

This affirmation of the VHP may confront restriction from the state government as Principal Secretary (Home) Devashish Panda had said that the Uttar Pradesh government would not permit entry of stones in Ayodhya for Ram Mandir.

"Since the issue is sub judice, the administration won't permit beginning of any new convention concerning Ayodhya issue," he had said.

(3) <u>Kesavananda Bharati vs State of Kerala, 1973</u>

Facts

His Holiness SripadGalvaru Kesavananda Bharati was head of a religious order in Kerala. The faction had certain terrains procured under its name. A portion of these grounds by the excellence of Kerala Land Reforms Act, 1963 which was additionally revised by Kerala Land Reforms (Amendment) Act, 1969 Ire to be obtained by the state government to satisfy their financial commitments. Hence, on 21st March 1970, the applicant moved to Apex Court u/a 32 for the requirement of rights under Articles 25 (Right to rehearse and proliferate religion), 26(Right to oversee religious issues), 14(Right to Equality), 19(1)(f) (Freedom to gain property), 31(Compulsory Acquisition of Property). In the meantime, when the request was under thought by the Court the State Government of Kerala passed Kerala Land Reforms (Amendment) Act, 1971.

After the phenomenal judgment of Golaknath v. Territory of Punjab, the edgy Parliament to pick up its lost amazingness and independence passed arrangement of Amendments to in a roundabout way overrule whatever was chosen in Golaknath{as talked about in Golaknath summary}. The Indira Gandhi govt. returned in the lower house with enormous lion's share in 1971 decisions and after that passed the 24th Amendment in 1971, 25th Amendment in 1972 and 29th Amendment in 1972.

24th Amendment

The Golaknath judgment set out that each change made under Article 368 will be hit by the special case set down in Article 13, accordingly to kill this the parliament through an alteration in Article 13 added proviso 4 by which any revision doesn't have any impact under Article 13.

To expel all or any trouble or vagueness the Parliament additionally added condition 3 to Article 368 which peruses as pursues… "Nothing in article 13 will apply to any revision made under this article."

In Golaknath the dominant part depended upon the Marginal note of the prior Article 368 to choose that the arrangement just contained the technique of Amendment and not control, consequently, the Marginal Note of Article 368 was corrected and word PoIr was included the Marginal Note.

Through a correction in Article 368(2) the parliament attempted to have any kind of effect between the strategy in alteration and common law. Prior the president had the decision to won't or retain the bill for the alteration yet after 24th Amendment he has no such decision to can't or retain the revision. Thusly the parliament attempted to make a correction and a conventional law unique to shield the revision from the special case referenced under a consolidated perusing of Article 13(1) and 13(3)(a).

25th Amendment

The parliament to explain their position that they are will undoubtedly enough repay the landowners altered Article 31(2) on the off chance that their property is procured by the state. "Amount" was put rather than pay in the arrangement.

Article 19(1)(f) was delinked from Article 31(2).

Article 31 C, another arrangement was added to the Constitution to expel all troubles that

I. Articles 14, 19 and 31 are not to be applied to any law authorized under the satisfaction of targets set down under Article 39(b) and 39(c).

II. Any law to offer impact to Article 39(b) and 39(c) will be inoculated from the court's mediation.

29th Amendment

The 29th Amendment goes in the year 1972 had the impact of embeddings The Kerala Land Reforms Act into IX Schedule which means it is outside the extent of legal investigation.

Since all these focal changes somehow spared the State corrections from being tested in official courtrooms, alongside the reproved arrangements of Kerala Land Reforms Act, legitimacy of 24th, 25th, and 29th Constitutional Amendments was additionally tested.

Issue

1. Constitutional Validity of 24th Constitutional (Amendment), Act 1971
2. Constitutional Validity of 25th Constitutional (Amendment), Act 1972
3. The extent of Parliament's power to amend the Constitution

Argument From PETITIONER'S Side

The candidate in the milestone case, entomb Alia, principally fought that the Parliament's capacity to change the Constitution is constrained and confined. This contention of prohibitive fitness with the Parliament depended on the Basic Structure hypothesis propounded by Justice Mudholkar in Sajjan Singh. The applicant through his advice argued under the watchful eye of the notable 13 judge seat to ensure his Fundamental Right to Property {then article 19(1)(f)} damaged by the institution of 24th& 25th Constitutional Amendment. The candidates additionally presented that it was the Constitution of India which conceded the resident's opportunity from oppression which they have endured on account of Colonialism. The different highlights of this opportunity will step by step wilt away if not shielded from the Parliament's ongoing course.

Argument From RESPONDENT'S Side

The respondent, for example, the State battled similar contentions which it has been fighting since Shankari Prasad, for example, the intensity of parliament concerning revising the Constitution is outright, boundless and free. This contention of the state depended on the essential standard of Indian Legal System, for example, Matchless quality of Parliament. Further, the state argued that to satisfy its financial commitments ensured to the natives by the association in Preamble, it is vital that there does not impede the expert of the Parliament. The embodiment of State's contentions was that on the off chance that what Golaknath and applicant are fighting turns into the law, at that point all the social and populist commitments gave on the Parliament by the most astounding law, for example, Constitution will come in direct genuine clash with the rights under Part III. The Respondents submitted under the watchful eye of the courts that even vote based system can be transformed into one gathering rule, if need be, by the Parliament.

Judgment

The court by a larger part of 7:6 held that Parliament can change any and each arrangement of the constitution subject to the condition that such alteration doesn't abuse Basic Structure of the constitution. The greater part choice was conveyed by S.M. Sikri CJI, K.S. Hegde, B.K. Mukherjea, J.M. Shelat, A.N. Grover, P. Jagmohan Reddy JJ. and Khanna J. agreeing with the greater part. While the minority suppositions Ire composed by A.N. Beam, D.G. Palekar, K.K. Mathew, M.H. Ask, S.N. Dwivedi and Y.V. Chandrachudjj. The minority seat however composing separate feelings, didn't surrender to the way that there are a few crucial arrangements. They Ire hesitant to concede total and liberated specialist to Parliament as for the intensity of change.

The 13 judges seat gave this milestone choice on 24 April 1973 (on the day when the then CJI S.M. Sikri was to resign). The court maintained whole 24th Constitutional (Amendment) Act, 1971 while it discovered the first piece of 25th Constitutional (Amendment) Act, 1972 intra vires &2nd part of the demonstration ultra vires. The court embracing social designing and adjusting the interests of the two prosecutors held that neither the Parliament can castrate Basic Structure of Constitution nor it can renounce the order to construct Ilfare state and a populist society. The court found the response to the inquiry left unanswered in Golaknathviz. the degree of revising poor with the Parliament. The appropriate response which the court concluded was DOCTRINE OF BASIC STRUCTURE. This regulation suggests that however, Parliament has the privilege to revise the whole Constitution yet subject to the condition that they can't in any way meddle with the highlights so key to this Constitution that without them it would be spiritless. To comprehend the substance of this precept it is of significance to comprehend Hegde and Mukherjeajj. who as they would like to think have perfectly clarified this Doctrine. As they would like to think the Indian Constitution is anything but a minor political archive rather it is a social report dependent on a social way of thinking. Each way of thinking like religion contains highlights that are essential and conditional. While the previous can't be adjusted the last can have changed quite recently like the guiding principle of religion can't change yet the practices related to it might change according to needs and necessities. The rundown of what comprises essential structure isn't thorough and the larger part seat has left it to the courts to decide these basic components. It is upon the courts to see that a specific change damages Basic structure or not. This inquiry must be considered for each situation with regards to a solid issue.

The real discoveries of the court are as per the following:

The court upon an incredible exchange and breaking down the issue finally found the intensity of Amendment as battled by the respondent in the reproved Article 368. After this judgment, the court made unequivocal what was understood pre-Golaknath.

The court in the wake of hearing the two sides arrived at the resolution that in actuality there do liesa contrast between common law and an alteration.

The Kesavananda Bharati case, to the degree of over two discoveries, overruled the Golaknath case. The judgment however overruling Golaknath didn't surrender total or liberated capacity to parliament as for Amendment in the Constitution. They held that however parliament can revise any and each arrangement of the Constitution subject to non-impedance and non-infringement of Basic Structure {Theory of Basic Structure}.

The seat likewise responded to the inquiry left unanswered by Golaknath about the degree of "Revision". The court found that "correct" in the arrangement of Article 368 represents a prohibitive undertone and couldn't credit to a key change. To comprehend it just; the parliament to pass an unavoidable legitimate change, the specific correction is liable to the utilization of Basic Structure test and needs to pass it.

Since the larger part decided that Parliament can change any and each arrangement of Constitution subject to Basic Structure test, it likewise had the impact of enabling Parliament to correct even FR's the length of they agree with the Basic Structure hypothesis.

The court recommended a couple of fundamental structures that they could find, for example, Free and Fair Elections, Supremacy of Constitution, Independent legal executive, Secularism, Federal Character of Nation, Separation of Polr, Republic and Democratic type of Government and so on. Be that as it may, the rundown they arranged isn't thorough and future courts on translation can include highlights they find as Basic Structures.

The larger part seat maintained the whole 24th Amendment Act legitimate though concerning 25th Amendment; it maintained 25th Amendment's first appendage and struck down the second However, this approval of 25th Amendment was liable to two conditions for example

I. Even though the court acknowledged that the exacting significance of "sum" isn't identical to remuneration and however courts can't continue choosing sufficiency of sum yet it can't be absurd and self-assertive. Neither the sum must be the market esteem however it ought to be sensibly identified with the market esteem.

II. The first piece of the Amendment was however maintained {delinking of Article 19(1)(f) from Article 31} yet the second part which banned legal reach was struck down. Khanna J. on this point opined that no law can bar the prosecutor to arrive at the courts for the implementation of their privileges.

The court in this way maintaining the first appendage of 25th Amendment gave the expected privilege to Parliament to satisfy their financial enactment ensured under Preamble just as in specific arrangements of Constitution and simultaneously spared the residents from Parliamentary Totalitarianism by striking down second appendage of the said correction since it banned the basic, legitimate and protected right of lawful cure.

The judgment of Kesavananda was an improvement over Golaknath in two terms;

I. The choice in Golaknath was confined uniquely to the security of Fundamental Rights from the self-governance of Parliament; in any case, Kesavananda widened its spread over every one of the arrangements that are key to the Constitution. Along these lines, the court in Kesavananda expanded the ambit of security of Constitution and impediment on Parliament's capacity.

II. The lion's share seat of Golaknath was of the supposition that the Parliament has no specialist to alter the Fundamental Rights and they Ire of the conclusion that to have an alteration, it needs to originate from the Constituent Assembly. This made Amendment too inflexible definition and unwittingly made the Constitution too delayed to even consider changing. Luckily, Kesavananda overruled Golaknath to this degree and alloId the adequate important adaptability to the Constitution.

Critical Analysis

The choice of the Kesavananda Bharati case was an interesting judgment. The seat in this choice after placing a ton of idea into it had thought of an extremely special. The choice running into more than 700 pages has contrived an answer applying which nor Parliament's commitments are upset and nor is there any plausibility of infringement of residents' Fundamental Right. Kesavananda is a great case of the legal arrangement were because of characteristic clash and equivocalness the Constitutional Machinery was fizzling. This inborn clash and uncertainty were settled when the lion's share seat thought of Doctrine of Basic Structure. This 13 judge seat choice revised wrong points of reference (Shankari Prasad, Sajjan Singh, Golaknath) made previously and exhibited the Indian Democracy where every one of the organizations borne through Constitution can play out their commitments agreeably. After the use of this choice Judiciary, as given by the Constitution, has turned out to be the last mediator to check infringement of sacred arrangements. Since Kesavananda Bharati case overruled Golaknath case it cleared the Parliament's approach to satisfy their commitments to make an Ilfare state and a libertarian culture. Alongside this, it has likewise put atop of confinement on the Parliament to hold its absolutism in line and to discover that there is no further infringement of Fundamental rights.

Kesavananda Bharati Case reflects the legal imagination of high request. The lion's share seat's choice to ensure the central highlights of the Constitution depended on sound and balanced thinking. The seat was frightful that if the Parliament is given unlimited altering poIr, at that point an ideological group with a two-third dominant part in Parliament, for a couple of years, could roll out any improvement in the Constitution even to the degree of revoking it to suit its inclinations. In any case, the seat was additionally aware of the destitution and social backwardness hiding in the country and to destroy this condition of neediness and social backwardness the Parliament would require a type of hardware. Hence, keeping both extraordinary conflicts in its brain, the court propounded Basic Structure hypothesis through which a fair Parliament can bring all the required changes required and simultaneously check a pernicious and polr covetous combination of government officials.

Conclusion

The Supreme Court perusing suggested restriction on Parliament's revising force was an intense and valiant move. The Constitution of India getting quality from national agreement and instituted for the sake of "Individuals of India" can't be revised by a minor 2/third dominant part when in all actuality 2/third larger part doesn't speak to the whole crowded of country, further it ought to be additionally remembered that not whole populace cast their particular votes in General Election. The strategy of Amendment requires the bill to go from both the houses and Rajya Sabha doesn't speak to individuals of India, for example, it's anything but an Ill known house thusly, it isn't altogether right to state that an Amendment gone by the houses speak to "Individuals of India".

Famous Jurist, amazing backer and co-counsel in Kesavananda Bharati Case, Nani Palkhiwala and the seven judges at greater part seat Ire of the sentiment that through this judgment they have spared Indian majority rule government which our regarded progenitors contended so energetically for. India after more than 150 years of battle got Independence from a provincial principle of Great Britain. The most significant result of this freedom was Democracy which gave average citizens (who Ire the most persecuted) polr and rights. If the seat had managed something else, these rights and polr for which our regarded political dissidents contended so energetically would have shrivelled away. Thusly, this valuable judgment had re-established the confidence of average citizens in Judiciary just as in Democracy.

(4) Maneka Gandhi v. Union Of India

Equivalent Citation - 1978 AIR 597, 1978 SCR (2) 621

Petitioner:

Maneka Gandhi

Respondent:

Union of India

Date of Judgment: 25/01/1978

BENCH:

Hameedullah Beg (CJI), Y.V.Chandrachud, P.N Bhagwati, V.R. Krishna Iyer, N.L.Untwalia,

 S.M. Fazal Ali& P.S.Kailasam

Background

The Supreme Court in Satwant Singh held that privilege to travel abroad is Ill inside the ambit of Article 21. In this way, to battle the above set down the law the Parliament ordered the Passports Act 1967. Identification Act, 1967 engages the specialists to appropriate the international ID of a certain individual if such activity is vital in light of a legitimate concern for sway and honesty of India, the security of India, agreeable relations of India with any remote nation, or the general public. The reasons of such impoundment are likewise to be imparted the influenced party anyway in light of a legitimate concern for the overall population these reasons can be withheld. In the prompt case, the experts on July fourth 1977 issued a notice of impoundment of the visa of Petitioner who was a referred to columnist referring to reasons as in light of a legitimate concern for the overall population. When the applicant got the notice of such appropriate she returned to the specialists asking for explicit nitty-gritty explanations behind what good reason her international ID will be seized. The specialists, in any case, addressed that the reasons are not to be determined in light of a legitimate concern for the overall population. In this way, the candidate moved toward Supreme Court u/a 32 for the requirement of Fundamental Right referenced u/a 14 against the discretionary activity of the specialists. The appeal was additionally revised and requirement of Article 21 for example Assurance of Life and Personal Liberty, Article 19(1)(a) for example Ideal to the right to speak freely of discourse and Article 19(1)(g) for example Appropriate to the opportunity of Movement. Among the significant reasons fought for the recording of such request, the applicant battled that the denounced request is told as it removed the solicitor's entitlement to be given a reasonable hearing to display her safeguard.

This case straightforwardly brought into inquiry the legitimateness and legitimacy of A.K. Gopalan v. Territory of Madras. All things considered, it was contended by the solicitor that whether the legitimacy of any law will be chosen by the way that it is a strategy built up by law or the law alongside being set up by law will likewise comply with standards of regular equity. The principle discussion was around the extent of "strategy set up by law" on the point that can such method be self-assertive or irrational or should it generally be simple, sensible and reasonable. The larger part seat anyway dismissing every one of the contentions of the solicitor held that the word law u/a 21 don't be in similarity with the standards of common equity. Be that as it may, it was Justice Fazal Ali's feeling for the situation that made ready for a liberal methodology of the understanding of Art. 21. Equity Fazal Ali disagreed with the larger part by holding that the privilege to life u/a 21 constitutes Principles of Natural Justice and the courts should watch that any methodology set up by law don't endure with the issue of irrationality and mediation. The soul of Justice Fazal Ali's contention was that the methodology ought to be simple, reasonable and sensible.

The court in Maneka Gandhi embraced the disagreeing perspective on Justice Fazal Ali in A.K. Gopalan v. Territory of Madras. In this manner, the court held that the while the system built up by law ought to be sensible, just and reasonable it will be free from any irrationality and assertion.

Issue

1. Is there any nexus between the provisions mentioned under Articles 14, 19 &21.
2. Scope of the word *"Procedure Established by Law."*
3. Whether a right to travel abroad resides in Article 21.
4. Whether a legislative law that takes away Right to life is reasonable.

Petitioner's Arguments

By the regulatory request of impoundment of the identification on fourth July 1977 the respondent has encroached Petitioner's Fundamental Right to Freedom of Speech and Expression, Right to travel abroad, Right to life and individual freedom and Right to the opportunity of development.

The arrangements of Article 14, 19 and 21 are to be perused in synchronization and they are not unrelated. These arrangements in itself however not expressly comprises in itself standards of characteristic equity. A consolidated perusing of the three arrangements will offer impact to the soul of the constitution and constitution creators.

Even though India has not embraced American "fair treatment of law" in its constitution, the method built up by law must be sensible, reasonable and simply free from any kind of mediation.

Area 10(3)(c) is violative of Article 21 of the constitution as in it abuses the privilege to life and individual freedom ensured under the said established arrangement. By the prudence of this arrangement, the solicitor was limited from voyaging abroad. This limit on the candidate was illegal since it was commonly acknowledged that privilege to travel abroad was inside the privilege to life and individual freedom u/a 21.

Audi Altrem Partem e. chance to be heard is all around perceived as a fundamental element of standards of common equity. These standards of characteristic equity locate no unequivocal spot in any sacred arrangements. Be that as it may, the soul of Fundamental Rights comprises in itself the quintessence of these standards. Further, Article 32 gives a chance to the influenced gatherings to straightforwardly approach Apex Court if there is any infringement of Part III arrangements. This arrangement of Article 32 was authored as Heart and Soul of the Constitution is proportionate to Audi Altrem Partem. Along these lines, it can't be said that the Principle of Natural Justice is discrete and elite to the Constitution.

Respondent's Arguments

The respondent battled under the steady gaze of the court that the international ID was seized because the candidate was required to show up before some councils for enquiry. The Attorney General additionally guaranteed the court to get rid of the considerable number of appearances in the said boards as quickly as time permits.

The respondent repeating the guideline set down in Gopalan fought that the word law u/a 21 can't be understood in the light central standards of common equity.

The respondent further fought that the standards of normal equity are dubious and brimming with ambiguities. In this manner, the constitution ought not to read such obscure and equivocal arrangements as a piece of it.

The ambit of Article 21 is wide and it, for the most part, contains the arrangements of Articles 14 and 19. In any case, any law must be named illegal to Article 21 when it straightforwardly encroaches Article 14 and 19.

Article 21 in its language contains "strategy built up by law" and such technique need not breeze through the assessment of sensibility. Further, the said arrangement need not be in similarity with Articles 14 and 19.

The constitution producers while drafting this constitution had bantered finally on American "fair treatment of law" and British "strategy set up by law". The obvious nonappearance of fair treatment of law from the Constitutional arrangements mirrors the brain of composers of this constitution. The brain and soul of the designers must be ensured and regarded.

Judgment

This milestone judgment Int ahead 25th January 1978 and changed the scene of the Constitution of India. This judgment extended the extent of Article 21 exponentially and this judgment genuinely and truly made India an Ilfare state as guaranteed in the Preamble. The seven-judge seat gave a consistent choice except certain judges agreeing on certain focuses.

There Ire seven separate suppositions in which the larger part assessment was composed by Justice Bhagwati for himself, Untwalia& Fazal Ali JJ. while Chandrachud, Iyer& Beg (CJ) composed separate however agreeing assessments.

The real discoveries of the court Ire as per the following:

The court while conveying this milestone judgment changed the scene of the Constitution by holding that however the expression utilized in Article 21 is "strategy built up by law" rather than "fair treatment of law" in any case, the system must be free from assertion and nonsensicalness.

Even though the Constitution producers must be regarded, yet they never planned to plant such a self – damaging bomb in the heart of the Constitution. They Ire never of the mind that the system need not be sensible, just and reasonable. They drafted this Constitution for the assurance of the "individuals of India" and such translation of Article 21 will be counter-beneficial to the insurance offered by the Constitution.

The court overruled Gopalan by expressing that there is a remarkable connection between the arrangements of Article 14, 19 and 21 and each law must breeze through the trial of the said arrangements. Prior in Gopalan, the larger part held that these arrangements in itself are fundamentally unrelated. In this way, to address its prior misstep the court held that these arrangements are not unrelated and subject to one another.

The court held that the extent of "individual freedom" isn't be interpreted in a thin and stricter sense. The court said that individual freedom must be comprehended in the more extensive and liberal sense. In this manner, Article 21 was given a broad understanding. The court committed the future courts to extend the skylines of Article 21 to cover all the Fundamental Rights and abstain from translating it in a smaller sense.

The privilege to travel abroad as held in Satwant Singh is inside the extent of certifications referenced under Article 21.

Segment 10(3)(c) of Passport Act 1967 isn't violative of neither Article 21 nor Article 19(1)(a) or 19 (1)(g). The court additionally held that the said 1967 arrangement likewise not in the logical inconsistency of Article 14. Since the said arrangement accommodates a chance to be heard. The court dismissed the dispute of candidate that the expression "in light of a legitimate concern for the overall population" isn't obscure.

The court held that Section 10(3)(c) and 10(5) is an authoritative request accordingly, open to challenge on the grounds of mala fide, absurd, disavowal of characteristic equity and ultra vires.

The court additionally proposed the government to customarily give reasons for each situation and should once in a while utilize the privilege of Section 10(5) of the 1967 demonstration.

The rights talked about under 19(1)(a) and 19(1)(g) is not kept to the regional furthest reaches of India.

Critical Analysis

The court in an admirable manner overruled the backward choice of Gopalan. The court by conveying this judgment has served everyday citizens. The court consistently came brutally upon the dispute of the respondent when it battled that the methodology built up by law need not be simple, reasonable and sensible. The respondent's contention that the law is substantial as long as it isn't revoked by the governing body. The court appropriately dismissed this broken contention of the respondent and gave the Right to Life and Personal Liberty another far-reaching and liberal elucidation.

The court held that however, the expression utilized in Article 21 is "system set up by law" rather than "fair treatment of law" notwithstanding, the technique must be free from intervention and mindlessness. The court likewise figured out how to regard and ensure the sacredness of the Constitution producers by this dark stain that the council was attempting to depict. The technique set up by law must fulfil certain necessities in the feeling of being sensible and just and it can't be subjective denying the natives the Fundamental rights.

The court likewise for the last time rested the discussion by holding that every Fundamental Right is not unmistakable from one another while they are commonly reliant on one another. In such a manner, Justice Iyer has very much opined that no Article in the Constitution is an island in itself. Bhagwati j. held that the procedural law needs to meet the prerequisites of Articles 14 and 19 to be a substantial law under Article 21.

Equity Iyer with regards to voyaging abroad held that "Travel makes freedom beneficial" consequently no individual can be denied of his entitlement to travel abroad.

The significance of Maneka Gandhi is boundless and how the zenith court got the chance to grow the skylines of Article 21 is exemplary. The advantages that collected to Indian natives can be very surely known by the consequence of Maneka Gandhi when courts start to embed each conceivable financial and social right in the extent of Article 21. The court in a catena of cases applying the proportion of this judgment has held Right to Clean Air, Right to Clean Water, Right to opportunity from Noise Pollution, Speedy Trial, Legal Aid, Right to Livelihood, Right to Food, Right to Medical Care, Right to Clean Environment[13]etc., as a piece of Right to Life and Personal freedom referenced u/a 21.

In all these above cases it is this judgment which has made ready for the courts to translate Article 21 out of a way which is helpful for the average citizens. The legal executive has through this judgment introduced another Iapon of satisfying the target set out in the Preamble in its stockpile.

Conclusion

The Maneka Gandhi judgment was reasonable and is perhaps the best judgment that the Indian Supreme Court has ever given. The judgment's most prominent element was the interlinking it set up between the arrangements of Article 14, 19 and 21. By the ethicalness of this connection, the court made these arrangements indivisible and a solitary substance. Presently any methodology to be substantial needs to meet every one of the prerequisites referenced under Article 14, 19 and 21. In this way, it extended the extent of individual freedom exponentially and secured the protected and central ideal to life all things considered.

The judgment while spared the residents from irrefutable activities of Executive additionally spared the sacredness of Parliamentary law when it didn't strike down Section 10(3)(c) and 10(5) of 1967 Act. The court likewise reminded the specialists to just once in a while utilize the right of segment 10(5) to fulfil that their activities Ire judicious and all-around idea. The court held that Section 10(3)(c) and 10(5) is an authoritative request in this way, open to challenge on the grounds of mala fide, outlandish, refusal of normal equity and ultra vires.

The judgment's significance can be seen today additionally because how the seat interpreted Article 21 and extended its points of view has given route for the settling of issues left unsolved by the Parliament. It's very clear that this judgment has assumed a basic job in interpreting Right to Clean Air, Right to Clean Water, Right to opportunity from Noise Pollution, Speedy Trial, Standard Education, Fair Trial, Legal Aid, Right to Livelihood, Right to Food, Right to Medical Care, Right to Clean Environment and so forth., as a piece of Right to Life and Personal freedom referenced u/a 21.

(5) <u>Mohd Ahmad Khan v. Shah Bano Begum</u>

Introduction

Mohd. Ahmad Khan V/S Shah Bano Begum is a milestone claim which has managed the issue of "Triple Talaq Verdict". This case is ordinarily referenced as "Shah Bano Case". It is viewed as a truly far from being a true and hazardous lawful challenge in India. This claim has substantiated to be an achievement in the battle of rights, an opportunity for the Muslim ladies.

It is about Shah Bano daring and valiant battle against the arrangement of Triple Talaq. Rather than making history or story of a smothered ladies she confronted the shame's of the network and her significant other. Even though she was confronting such an uncommon circumstance in her life she chose to battle against her significant other and confronted the existence where everybody was agreeable to her better half, or more all she courageously chose to battle against the male-overwhelmed society. She battled against the arrangement of Triple Talaq and finally her endeavours not Int futile, she had the option to accomplish what she needed and has changed the framework forever.

Facts

- In 1932, Shah Bano was hitched to Mohd. Ahmad khan, who was a prestigious legal counsellor in Indore.

- They Ire the guardians of 3 children and 2 little girls for example in absolute they have 5 youngsters.

- After 14 yrs. Of their marriage, Shah Bano's better half Added another ladies who were more youthful than him.

- In 1975, when Shah Bano age was of 62 yrs, she was abandoned by her significant other and was tossed out from her Adding home alongside her youngsters.

- In April 1978, she brought an intrigue under Sec. 125 of code of the criminal system, 1973 (CrPC) within the sight of a legal judge of Indore after when she was discarded from her Adding home by her significant other.

- Shah Bano filed this suit in 1978 because her significant other has deserted her from the support of Rs. 200 every month which he ensured to give.

- A spouse who is with no pay and is disregarded by her significant other qualifies for upkeep, which incorporates a separated from a wife who isn't remarried.

- In Nov. 1978, he offered separation to his significant other Shah Bano by articulating or expressing "Triple Talaq and it was irreversible.

- The contention or struggle betweenShah Bano's youngsters and her better half's other spouse Ire essential reason or grounds on which separation was surrendered and outfitted.

- After he articulates unavoidable Triple Talaq, he took a shield that since due to this separation she has been ended to be her legitimate spouse and because of which he was not responsible to outfit her with upkeep or provision.

- The nearby court (justice) court coordinated Mohd. Ahmad to outfit her Rs. 25 every month to Shah Bano in a type of upkeep.

- Shah Bano in July 1908, aside from this, made supplication to High Court of M.P, to modify the measure of support to Rs. 179 consistently.

- Shah Bano's point of reference Int to Supreme Court and filed an appeal against the decision of High Court of Madhya Pradesh.

- Her better half fundamental contention after separation he can't keep any type of partnership or association with his separation spouse since it isn't permitted by Islamic laws/Islam and is "Haram" and henceforth he isn't lawfully capable to keep up her significant other.

Issues Raised In This Case:-

- Whether Section 125 of the Code Of Criminal Procedure is worried about Muslims or not.
- Whether the measure of Mehr given by the spouse on separation is sufficient to get the husband free and is at risk to keep up his significant other or not.
- whether the Uniform Civil Code applies to all religions or not.

Judgment:-

- The decision of the Shah Bano case was passed on by C.J, CHANDRACHUD.
- All India Muslim Personal Law Board and Jamiat ulema-e-Hind Ire the two Muslim Bodies Int with the claim as an intervenor.
- On 3rdFeb. 1981, the Supreme Court gave a similarly invested end for this situation and exiled the request of Mohd. Ahmad Khan and approve the decision of the High Court.
- The court held that Section 125of Code Of Criminal Procedure requested to Muslims as Ill, with no looked for of segregation.
- Supreme Court for this situation properly held that since the duty of Muslim spouse towards her separated from the wife is constrained to the degree of " Iddat" period, even though this circumstance doesn't mull over the standard of law that is referenced in Section 125 of CrPc.,1973
- According to the Supreme Court, this standard as indicated by Muslim Law was against humankind or wasn't right because here a separated from a spouse was not in a condition to look after herself.
- Thus toward the end, after an extremely long method court, at last, inferred that the spouse is lawful risk will arrive at an end whenever separated from the wife is skilled to look after herself.
- But this circumstance will be turned around for the situation when a spouse isn't capable in a condition to back or keep up herself after the Iddat time frame, she will qualify to get support or divorce settlement under Section 125 of CrPc.

Muslim Women (Protection Of Rights On Divorce) Act, 1986:-

The judgment given in Shah Bano Case was scrutinized among Muslims and as per them this choice was in strife with the guidelines of "Quran" and "Islamic Laws/Islam". So Parliament of India in 1986, (Congress govt.) chose to order the Muslim ladies (Protection Of Rights Of Divorce) Act, 1986. The fundamental goal of this demonstration was to secure the privilege of the separated from Muslim ladies and additionally to the individuals who have separate from their husband's.

The institution of this demonstration was finished by the legislature of Rajiv Gandhi, to refute the choice/order gone by Supreme Court in Shah Bano Begum case. As per this demonstration, Muslim separated from ladies ought to qualify for sufficient and sensible measure of upkeep till the Iddat time frame. At the point when a separated from ladies keeps up a youngster conceived by her whenever previously or after the separation, the spouse is under legitimate commitment to give a specific measure of upkeep for the tyke to a time of 2 yrs. From the birth date of a tyke. The ladies are likewise approved to acquire "Mahr" or "doer" and get back every one of the properties or bequest which is given to her by her folks, companions, relatives, spouse or husband's companions. On the off chance that such focal points are not gotten by the separated from Muslim ladies from her previous spouse, she can apply to an officer for requesting him to give her support/divorce settlement or measure of "Mahr" or doer or her bequest or properties.

Critical Analysis:-

On account of Mohd. Ahmad Khan V/S Shah Bano Begum, the Supreme Court explicitly underlined the that Triple Talaq can't remove the upkeep right of a separated from Muslim ladies who aren't in a condition to keep up herself or her kids when she is repudiated or separated by her significant other. The period when the decision of Shah Bano Case was conveyed by the Supreme Court it confronted a great deal of analysis. By then of time Muslim ladies climate Added or unmarried Ire not given opportunity even they Ire suspended from that point essential opportunity, which is against humankind and it essentially damages the essential or key privileges of people. Muslim ladies Ire in reverse in there status when contrasted with other ladies of the world. They Ire not instructed and confident when contrasted with other ladies. They confronted difficult issues and issues which prompted the abatement in their degree of self-assurance and their insight in different orders. Alongside these things they Ire not permitted to think about or teach themselves and they Ire likewise denied to work either. Since they confronted every one of these things from their very youth it was exceptionally common that they in their troublesome time can't gain their living and can keep up themselves so for them, support or upkeep was genuinely necessary.

Shah Bano case was an ordinary case simply like different instances of upkeep which has occurred and the decision that was finished up by Supreme Court was likewise like the past claims yet the two bare truth that was seen for this situation put forth this defence a milestone judgment case and the two bare truth was-right off the bat, otherworldliness of religious individual laws was censured and afterwards it was addressed whether Uniform Civil Code is applied to all religion and their adherents and also, regardless of whether CrPc is applied to individual religious laws.

Conclusion:-

This was the situation of a Triple Talaq decision which as per me was a memorable decision as it keeps up reality and confidence of the individuals in the legal executive as for this situation, "Equity and balance has beaten religion". As per me, this claim was an achievement in the legal executive as it was a gallant, intense, fair and special choice. This judgment has denoted the significance of support which ought to be given to the separated from Muslim ladies who are not in the condition to gain and look after themselves.

Even though the decision of the Shah Bano case given by the Supreme Court was negated by the support of Muslim Women Act, the court held in the further decision's that separated from Muslim. ladies, under Section 125 of CrPc can certify support or provision from their previous spouse, or separated from this separated from Muslim ladies can declare or guarantee for round some cash or sum under Muslim Women Act. The Supreme Court even though after grimy governmental issues passed the fair judgment and finally it had kept up the trust and confidence of natives in the legal executive.

Introduction

This case is frequently alluded to as the dark spot on the Indian Judiciary since this judgment had seeping outcomes on the life and freedom of a resident of India. The outcomes Ire with the end goal that even today the detestations of the violent occasions of India get reflected at whatever point a reference is made to this specific case. During the 1970s when the crisis was forced every one of the foundations of the nation Ire profoundly politicized and energized and even the Supreme Court of India was not left immaculate from the equivalent.

Facts

Indira Gandhi's political decision was tested in the Allahabad High Court and the court requested against Indira Gandhi indicting her for the offences of improper practices to win the political decision. Frantic to keep the post of Prime Minister, she mentioned the then President of India to force a crisis in the nation. Accordingly, a crisis was forced on 27.06.1975 under A. 359 (1) of the constitution and the request forcing the crisis which suspended A 14, A21 and A22 of the constitution of India. A few people Ire unlawfully imprisoned, confined and put in the slammer who restricted the moves of the Prime Minister. Accordingly, a few people moved the High Courts under the arrangements of Article 226 of the Constitution of India to verify the freedom of their friends and family by method for utilizing the Writ of Habeas Corpus which gives alleviation when somebody is unlawfully confined The High Courts offered alleviation to such people and liberate them. Notwithstanding, this was not preferred by the decision heads and the State recorded petitions in the Supreme Court testing the sets of the High Courts whereby people Ire liberated.

Issues

The main issue before the Court was that when an emergency was imposed under the provisions of the constitution and when the A. 14, A. 21 and A.22 had been suspended then can a writ of Habeas Corpus be maintainable in front of the court and can relief be granted to an individual.

Petitioners Arguments

It was contended by the State that the primary point of the arrangements of the crisis was that they vest uncommon pores in the official to hold unlimited oversight over the peace of the nation since a crisis circumstance is of outrageous significance when the circumstance is fragile. It was additionally contended that when an individual had been confined it couldn't be tested that the request for detainment wasn't right and that there Ire no solid motivations to keep an individual. At the point when a crisis is declared an individual relinquishes A. 19 of the Constitution and if an individual is held in repudiation of the A. 22 of the Constitution the equivalent can't be addressed in a procedure of Habeas Corpus since the alternative to appeal to the court is shut during the crisis. It was battled that the abbreviation of such a privilege was done under the arrangements of the constitution and a President's Order can't be addressed. A presidential request under A. 359 is made under extraordinary conditions and in this manner, it was not open for the court to scrutinize the justification behind the equivalent and engage a Habeas Corpus request.

Respondents Arguments

The respondents contended that the object of A. 359 was to evacuate any sort of abbreviation on the intensity of the lawmaking body from enacting during the crisis. The article disallows moving to the Supreme Court for authorizing certain rights yet there was no denial on moving to the High Court under A 226 for upholding statutory privileges of individual freedom. It was additionally battled that the presidential request was against the rule of normal law and other basic essential standards of law. At the point when there was a law which managed preventive detainment then the equivalent must fit in with the conditions set out by the law. It was likewise battled that Article 21 was not the sole holder of the privilege to life and individual freedom. There Ire rights which Ire not key rights but rather statutory or regular rights. These rights Ire not influenced by the Presidential Order and couldn't be removed. It was additionally contended that where the state had made a law for making detainments then the detainments ought to be inside the limits and states of the rule. On the off chance that the conditions Ire not met, at that point the detainment would go past the intensity of the state.

Judgment

This case was heard by five judges of the Supreme Court of India. Four of the five judges ruled in favour of the state and held that during an emergency the fundamental rights Ire not available to a citizen. All rights will be extinguished in light of the presidential order. It was further held that an individual would not have the option of moving the High Court for a Writ of Habeas Corpus if the Presidential Order said so and all the proceedings in the court will remain suspended till the duration of the emergency. One judge (J) H.R. Khanna, however, gave a dissenting judgment i.e., a view was taken against the finding of the majority judgment and this is regarded in today's times the correct view and the best descent. It paved the way for the future development of the Law. He held that during an emergency under A. 359 even if a fundamental right is taken away, a person can move the court for the enforcement of his statutory right. He was of the view that A. 21 is not the only place for life and liberty. Even if it is taken away the right to life and personal liberty are the basic tenets of society. The State cannot deprive a person of his life and personal liberty without the authority of law.

(7) <u>INA Trial</u>

INA (Indian National Army) was a pair that involved Indian Prisoners of War abroad and was shaped by Subhash Chandra Bose to verify India's freedom from the British. When it was disbanded, INA's top officials Ire attempted by the British on charges of Sedition and so on. The Indian National Congress chose to shape a group of lawful stalwarts to set up an intensive legitimate resistance for the officials. Master Wavell India's then Viceroy, proclaimed a law with review impact to present ward on court-martials in cases identified with Pows.

The apex of this preliminary was the lawful resourcefulness shown by Bhulabhai Desai. Desai's essential contention was that Bose had shaped a temporary administration of India, and since the Axis forces had perceived that legislature, the officials of the INA are speaking to their nation, and not an agitator more. Therefore, Desai contended, the civil law for this situation, the Indian Penal Code was not material and they should be attempted under International Law. He set tremendous proof on record to set up that the INA was speaking to the Indian State; and along these lines, the officials Ire acting in the facilitation of their obligation as India and Great Britain Ire at war. Even though he lost the case, he earned his place in the pantheon of legends.

<h3 align="center">(8) <u>Bhawal case – The Princely Imposter</u></h3>

The Bhawal Sanyasi case has been one of the most unusual among legal cases in British India. In the Hindu lifestyle, a Sanyasi is an individual who has taken 'Sanyas' or entered the last phase of his life wherein he is to look for the Truth and turn his back upon the material world. In the progressively prevalent speech, any commonplace sadhu or homeless person might be known as a sanyasi. Bhawal was a huge zamindari close to Dacca (presently Dhaka, Bangladesh). It was, likewise with the instance of numerous comparable Zamindaries, firmly administered by the British organization. It had an Englishman as a chief. After the Zamindar kicked the bucket, it goes to his three children. All drove lives of simplicity. The subsequent child, Ramendra, passed on in Darjeeling in 1905, clearly because of syphilis, and was accepted to have been incinerated. He left his widow, Bibhavati, behind him. Quite a long while later, in 1921, a Sadhu should up in Dacca. Before long individuals saw numerous similarities among him and the probably dead Ramendra. Jyotirmayee, one of his sisters was persuaded that the sadhu was, in reality, her sibling. A few instructed Indians also Ire persuaded of his personality. The British authority world, then again, vield him as a faker. Bibhavati would not acknowledge him as her significant other. The inquirer (sadhu) asserted his 1/third share from the incomes of the zamindari. The Court of Wards which was overseeing the zamindari declined the case and the issue Int to the court. From the earliest starting point, there was a reasonable division between the British officialdom and the Bengali tip-top, the last agreeing with the petitioner. The petitioner recorded a suit in 1930.

The judgment in the principal preliminary Int for the petitioner. The Court of Wards spoke to the Calcutta High Wards. After some deferral brought about constantly World War, which kept one of the allotted judges stranded in London, the High Court excessively found for the inquirer in 1940. Bibhavati spoke to the Privy Council in London. The Privy Council decided for the petitioner on July 30, 1946. The judgment was transmitted to Calcutta the following day.

That very day the champ/inquirer Int to the Kali sanctuary to offer petitions upon his triumph and endured a stroke there. He kicked the bucket two days after the fact, which, as indicated by Bibhavti, was the supernaturally appointed discipline for the faker.

This case was as of late referenced in the Anna Hazare hostile to defilement development when Section 144 of the IPC (unlawful gathering) was forced by the Delhi Police and the legal advisor group of Shanti and Prashant Bhushan contended effectively in the Supreme Court over the illegal idea of this activity. The first case managed a typical native's entitlement to hold open gatherings on boulevards and the degree to which the state could direct this right. The opportunity of articulation and gathering is a basic component of popularity based framework. At the base of this framework lies the natives' entitlement to meet eye to eye to talk about issues social, religious or political. This privilege was maintained for this situation.

Deciding looking into the issue that had been recorded by the vanquished restriction up-and-comer Raj Narain, Justice Jagmohan Lal Sinha announced then-PM Indira Gandhi liable of constituent misbehaviours, negated her success from Rae Bareilly and banned her from holding chose office for a long time. The choice caused a political tempest in India that prompted the burden of a highly sensitive situation by Indira's administration from 1975 to 1977. The choice hosted stirred restriction gatherings and strikes by workers and worker's guilds, understudy associations and government associations cleared the nation over. Challenges driven by Jayaprakash Narayan and Morarji Desai overwhelmed the lanes of Delhi near the Parliament building and the Prime Minister's living arrangement. The legislature contended that the political issue was a risk to national security. Utilizing the general forces conceded by the Emergency order, a huge number of restriction pioneers and activists Ire captured, press control was presented and races Ire deferred. During this period,

Indira Gandhi's Congress (R) utilized its parliamentary lion's share to change the Indian Constitution and overwrite the law that she was later discovered blameworthy of abusing.

(11)   <u>Lal Bihari, The Undead Indian</u>

In 1976, when an adolescent named Lal Bihari moved toward a bank to affirm an advance, he was educated that he was in reality dead. It took Lal Bihari 18 years to recover his life and his territory. During that time, he included the word Mritak or Dead, to his name and to demonstrate that he was alive looked for capture, attempted to keep running for parliament, abducted the child of his uncle, who had taken his property, undermined murder, offended judges, tossed pamphlets posting his grumblings at lawmakers in the state get together and requested a widow's annuity for his significant other. Each time he was either whipped by police or reproached for burning through authorities' time. Unfit to make progress, Lal Bihari, The Dead looked for the organization of different phantoms in Uttar Pradesh and found a whole black market of the perished and seized. It was uniquely in 1994, 18 years after being pronounced dead, that Azamgarh locale justice, a Hausa Prasad Verma, announced Lal Bihari at long last alive by and by and restored his territory to him.

(12)   <u>The state of Orissa v. Ram Bahadur Thapa (1959)</u>

This is a peculiar one. Slam Bahadur Thapa was the worker of one J.B. Chatterjee of Chatterjee Bros. firm in Calcutta. They had come to Rasogovindpur, a town in Balasore locale in Orissa to buy zero scraps from a surrendered aerodrome outside the town. Since it was relinquished, local people trusted it was spooky. This aroused the interest of Chatterjee who needed to "see the phantoms". Around evening time, as they 're advancing toward the aerodrome they saw a glinting light inside the premises which, because of the solid breeze, appeared to move. They thought it was will-o'- the-wisp. Thapa took decisive action as he released his khukuri to assault the "apparitions". Turns out, they are nearby Adivasi ladies with a tropical storm lamp who had accumulated under a Joshua tree to gather a few blossoms. Thapa's aimless hacking caused the passing of one Delhi Majhiani and harmed two other ladies. The Sessions court judge nonetheless, cleared Thapa pronouncing that his activities Ire the aftereffect of a stern faith in apparitions and that at the time, Thapa accepted that they Ire legitimately defended.

(13)   <u>Mathura Rape Case (1972)</u>

This is one of the most significant cases in the nation, because the dissents that pursued the decision, constrained some significant changes in assault laws in India. Mathura, a youthful inborn lady, was assaulted by two constables inside the premises of the Desai Ganj Police Station in Chandrapur area of Maharashtra. The Sessions court judge found the denounced not blameworthy. The thinking behind this was (in all honesty) that Mathura was habituated to sex. This, as per the judge, unmistakably suggested that the sexual demonstration in the police headquarters was consensual. The revisions to the law that Ire constrained by the dissents made one thing right - accommodation doesn't mean assent.

(14)   <u>NALSA vs Union of India (2014)</u>

This is the landmark decision by the Supreme Court of India which declared that Transgendered People Ire the 'third gender' and that they had equal rights as any other gender. The petitioner, in this case, was the National Legal Services Authority (NALSA).

(15)   Bhawal Case (1921-1946)

It's still viewed as one of India's most abnormal personality cases. It, for the most part, spun around a conceivable impostor who professed to be the ruler of Bhawal Estate, one which involved more than 2000 towns and was one of unified Bengal's biggest zamindari bequests. Ramendra, the second Kumar of the Bhawal bequest passed on in the mid-twentieth century, yet there Ire bits of gossip about him not so much being dead. After ten years, in 1921, a sanyasi who looked a great deal like Ramendra was discovered meandering the lanes of Dhaka. For reasons unknown, the previous inhabitants and ranchers of Ramendra vouched for this man and upheld his case to the title. Nearly everybody aside from Ramendra's widow, Bibhabati, trusted him. There was a long lawful procedure including two preliminaries where the two sides endeavoured to demonstrate their cases. Meanwhile, the new Ramendra additionally moved to Calcutta and where he was invited in the tip-top circles. He used to routinely gather 1/third of the home income, which was his offer. He utilized that cash to help his way of life while likewise paying the lawful charges of the case. At last, in 1946, the court at long last governed to support him, yet not long after that, he passed away because of a stroke he had endured a few days sooner.

(16)   Tarakeswar Case (1874)

This case was so (for the absence of a superior word) 'Ill known', that specialists needed to offer tickets to give individuals a chance to come inside the sessions court. Furthermore, the story itself is a blockbuster. Nobin Chandra cut the throat of his 16-year old spouse, Elokeshi, who was having an unsanctioned romance with the mahant of the neighbourhood Tarakeswar sanctuary. Even though Nobin Chandra gave himself over to the police and admitted his wrongdoing, local people Ire for the most part on his side. The police needed to release him following two years, even though he was serving an actual existence detainment while the mahant was captured and put in a correctional facility for a long time. Then again, there Ire likewise gossipy tidbits that the mahant had assaulted Elokeshi on the guise of helping her out with "richness issues". This case was extremely significant for that timeframe because this was seen by the general public as one of those minutes where the British rulers intruded in the issues of the Bengali bhadralok and a sanctuary cleric, something that was exceptionally uncommon back then.

Before the Vishakha Guidelines came in, the working environment was perilous for some ladies particularly if there should arise an occurrence of lewd behaviour. In 1992, Bhanwari Devi was assaulted by upper station men in her town since she attempted to bring up her voice against tyke marriage. Because of gross carelessness, the vaginal swabs gathered from her body Ire taken 48 hours after the occurrence. In a perfect world, it ought to be done as such inside 24 hours. Amazingly, the judge directing her case (this was the seventh judge after six others Ire evacuated) vindicated the charged, notwithstanding going so far to state, " Since the guilty parties Ire upper-position men and incorporated a brahmin, the assault couldn't have occurred because Bhanwari was from a lower standing. " Following the shock over this quittance, Vishakha and some other ladies' gatherings documented a PIL against the State of Rajasthan and the Union of India, driving the last to receive the Vishakha Guidelines which presently secures working ladies everywhere throughout the nation.

****

www.ingramcontent.com/pod-product-compliance
Lightning Source LLC
Chambersburg PA
CBHW081634250726
48657CB00009B/2873